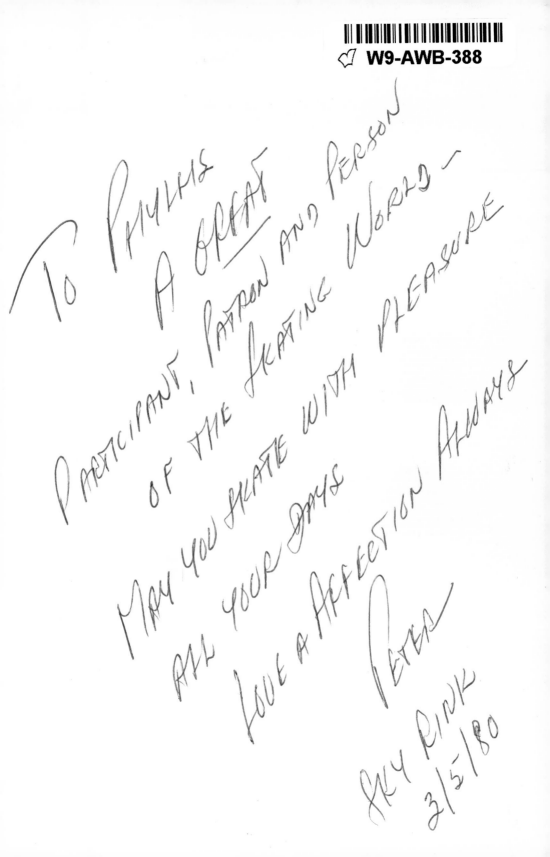

To Phyllis
A GREAT
Participant, Patron and Person
of the Skating World —
May you skate with pleasure
all your days

Love & Affection Always

Peter

Sky Rink
3/5/80

ICE SKATING
FOR EVERYBODY

Ice skating is available today in places famous and not-so-famous, indoors as well as outdoors. Credit: Rockefeller Center, New York.

ICE SKATING FOR EVERYBODY

Your Self-Teaching Guide

By Peter Dunfield
and
Irwin J. Polk, M.D.

Photos by Kenn Duncan
and Irwin J. Polk

David McKay Company, Inc.
New York

Contents

Introduction

For excitement, there is nothing quite like skating. The feeling of motion, combined with the sense of control over your body in activity, is unlike that of any other sport. Skating gives a combination of feelings: the feeling of freedom and motion found in flying and gliding, the sensation of leaning motion found in bike riding and surfing, the flow of motion and the smoothness and change of direction enjoyed in skiing on snow or on water. The skater can use the speed of a sprinter and the quickness and maneuverability of a basketball player. He or she can develop the conditioning of a miler with the precision of a springboard diver. The skater can feel the body contact of football or basketball or the rhythm of a gymnast.

Skating can provide all of these elements. The hockey player enjoys one of the best contact sports. Speed skaters develop explosive power and endurance. Grace and precision come with figure skating.

But best of all, perhaps, is the fun and stimulation, the change of pace available to the pleasure skater in the clean, sparkling world of ice.

Skating has attracted millions of people to the ice all over the world. In the United States, skating is on the brink of a fantastic expansion. Through television, the public has been exposed to hockey, speed skating, and figure skating. People are being attracted to the ice in such large numbers that the number of ice rinks in the United States alone has grown from 500 to about 1,500 since 1960. Most of these rinks have been built and operated as small businesses, but about half are publicly owned and operated. The demand has led to the building and operating of rinks by city and county governments for community recreational activities.

More than 20 million Americans skate. There are more than 60 million paid rink admissions yearly in the United States. Recreational skaters have indeed taken to the ice.

Hockey is undergoing a tremendous expansion, too. There are more than 100,000 registered players in the some 500 hockey clubs in organized amateur hockey in the United States. In addition, professional hockey has a wide television audience. More than 300 schools and colleges now include hockey in their athletic programs. This expansion is not confined to the United States. Sweden has more than 160,000 registered hockey players, and the number in Russia is a staggering 3 million.

Who can skate? Anyone who can stand on skates can skate in them. Children as young as four or five can master the essentials of skating. Older children, teenagers, and young adults learn readily. It is possible to learn to skate comfortably even after age sixty-five.

Boys can skate; girls can skate. After learning the basics, they can select the kind of skating they enjoy most. Hockey and speed skating are often the thing for boys, but many girls enjoy them, too. Figure skating seems to attract more girls than boys, but some of the finest figure skaters are boys. Adults may find fun in any kind of skating. Perhaps the largest group of skaters are the recreational skaters who just get out and do their thing on the ice.

Skating, once strictly a wintertime sport, can now be enjoyed year-round. Because of the development of new techniques of ice making and air conditioning, the pleasures of skating can now be enjoyed indoors or out throughout the year in most climates. In Sun Valley, Idaho, there is outdoor skating even in July.

Indoor rinks such as this one (Sky Rink in New York City) make it possible to enjoy ice skating throughout the year.

How to Use This Book

This book is a self-teaching course in the basics of skating. It has been designed to take the beginner from the first steps on ice to the point where specialized skating begins for any of the three main areas: 1) hockey, 2) speed skating, or 3) figure skating.

This teaching system is useful for beginners of any age group. As a rule, children feel more comfortable with new physical activities than adults, and learn them faster. Nevertheless, adults, too, can begin at any age and, by following this combination of text and photos, learn how to skate.

This book can also be used by parents who skate, to organize their own knowledge about skating for teaching their younger children. Older children can use this book by themselves.

A warning, though: do not take the book onto the ice with you. A new skater has enough difficulty learning the basics without the additional problem of holding a book and trying to read at the same time. Instead, read each lesson over carefully before you go out onto the ice. Work on only a small portion at a time. When you have any questions, leave the ice and refer to the book.

As you progress, it will be important to review on the ice all of the previous lessons each time you begin to skate. This review will serve two purposes: 1) it will provide you with a needed warm-up on the ice and 2) it will help you recall what you have learned and thereby reinforce your learning. Your ability to skate will increase rapidly with repeated practice of the things you have already learned.

How quickly should you progress? At your own speed. Make sure you understand each technique before moving on to the next. Do not become discouraged if you have some difficulty doing some of the exercises. These exercises have been arranged

1

in a logical sequence, building from one to the next. You should attempt to go further in the study plan only when you feel comfortable with your accomplishments up to that point. Plan to learn the skills taught here in one season of regular skating twice a week.

Remember that this book is intended to explain only the basic elements of skating. Further specialized learning in hockey, speed skating, or figure skating may require lessons from a friend or a skating pro.

After you learn the fundamentals described in this book, you may wish to choose further instruction in a specialty like the young hockey players at a clinic in Sun Valley (top) or the aspiring figure skaters (above) in a training session with Peter Dunfield at Sky Rink in New York City.

Where Did It All Begin?

Skating began in the colder climates of northern Europe. The first skates were bone runners bound to shoes with leather thongs. The first metal runners date from about A.D. 300 in Scandinavia. These gradually evolved into our present-day blade of fine tempered steel.

Skating was introduced into Britain with the Anglo-Saxon invasion of about A.D. 450. Wooden skates with leather facing appeared in the fourteenth century. About two hundred years later, skating appeared as a basic mode of transportation in the Netherlands. Famous paintings by sixteenth-century Flemish and Dutch artists portray canals in the Low Countries swarming with skaters of all ages. The Dutch in particular used skates for transportation, to carry their goods to market. They also skated to school and to church.

But skating was not only for such workaday activity. Throughout northern Europe, rulers from the time of Charles II of England have enjoyed the thrill of skating. Queen Victoria's interest in skating led to the development of skating at all levels of society in her day.

But an even more significant boost in the popularity and acceptance of skating came with the development of the artificially frozen indoor rink. The first such rink was built in Chelsea, England, in 1876. It was twenty-four feet by forty feet, about one fourth the size of a present-day hockey rink. With the development of the indoor rink, skating was able to escape the dependency on seasonal and daily weather conditions. Eventually, through the availability of artificial ice, skating could become the year-round pastime it is today.

3

Hockey as we know it came into being about ten years after the first artificial rink was built. Hockey originated in Kingston, Ontario, Canada, in 1885. The sport may well have developed from an old Indian game.

At about the same time, a great American skater—Jackson Haynes—freed the sport of figure skating from its emphasis on printing formal patterns on the ice. His "Continental style" of skating captured world enthusiasm by introducing balletlike free movements, including jumps and spins to the ice. In the 1930s, Olympic Champion Sonja Henie popularized skating for the general public. After winning the Olympic titles in 1928, 1932, and 1936, she went on to introduce skating to the public through a series of motion pictures and spectacular ice shows. Today the ice-show spectacular provides family entertainment throughout the world.

Another Olympic Champion, the great American athlete Dick Button, further advanced the techniques of jumping and spinning on ice. In recent years, as a TV commentator he has made millions of viewers familiar with the beauty and excitement of competitive figure skating.

Peggy Fleming, perhaps the best-known woman skater of recent times, is credited with reestablishing the supremacy of Americans in figure skating after a plane crash in 1961 killed the entire American world-competition team and coaches. Miss Fleming was presented in a series of highly popular TV specials to rekindle the interest and reaffirm the glamor of skating for the American public. She demonstrated the application to the ice of precise, smooth, balletic movement.

The most recent American Olympic skating champion, Dorothy Hamill, successfully combined poised vigor with well-defined athletic movement to enchant millions at the 1976 Olympics and later on TV specials.

Hockey has also become familar to millions of television fans. Inspired by such stalwarts as Bobby Hull and the Howe family, hundreds of hockey schools and clinics have been developed throughout North America. Television and these clinics have been responsible for hockey's fantastic growth as a spectator and participant sport in recent years.

Even speed skating has expanded in the United States lately. Although earliest records date from the 1700s, it was not until the past decade, when speed tracks became more widely available, that speed skating attracted much attention. The success in the 1972 Olympics of two American girls, Ann Henning and Diane Holum, stimulated much interest in speed skating, particularly among girls and women.

Where to Skate

Skating can be done any place that ice is available. For centuries, of course, skating was done only out-of-doors on naturally frozen rivers, lakes, and ponds. When the conditions are ideal, skating out-of-doors on a frozen, natural body of water provides the skater with a matchless experience of freedom, expansiveness, and harmony with nature.

But outdoor conditions are seldom ideal, so it is not surprising that the growth of interest in skating in the country has paralleled the development of artificially frozen indoor rinks. Indoor ice has many advantages over natural outdoor ice, especially for a beginner. It provides consistent conditions, uniform ice, and controlled temperature, plus the security of knowing that you will not take a sudden plunge into frigid water. Furthermore, good skates are available to rent at most ice rinks, and qualified instruction can be arranged.

Rinks that are privately owned offer public sessions lasting two to two-and-one-half hours for about the price of a movie. In some areas, rinks operated by the county or city are likely to charge slightly less, and their use may be restricted to residents. Ordinarily, the private rinks offer somewhat more elaborate facilities and services, perhaps including skate rental and food concessions. Usually the availability and quality of instruction in skating is a bit better at the privately owned facilities.

Studios and small skating-school rinks also provide indoor ice. They usually feature teaching programs, but may also provide limited public-session time. Studios and skating-school rinks are particularly popular with students, since they offer practice in uncrowded conditions and an enthusiastic atmosphere.

If there is no indoor rink nearby, you can learn to skate out-doors. Skating there is usually most invigorating, but it does not always offer the best conditions for learning. Fighting the cold, the wind, and the irregular ice can be exhausting. But when conditions are good, outdoor skating can be the most pleasurable skating of all. Look for a pond that is sheltered from the wind by tall trees or a steep bank. Without the wind, skating will be more comfortable and the ice will be a bit smoother.

You can tell a good bit about the suitability of the ice by its appearance. Ice thickness of two or three inches over a shallow pond after a quick freeze is ideal. Black or dark green ice is best, very elastic and quite safe. White ice, on the other hand, contains much air and is therefore quite brittle and very dangerous. It will crack and shatter suddenly and widely, especially in rising temperature. The appearance of diagonal cracks through which water can be seen creating more cracks and little triangles suggests rippled, unsafe ice that should be avoided.

Enter the ice from the south side of the pond. This side is the side least subject to sunlight and so it's where the ice will tend to be firmest. As with swimming, never skate alone on outdoor ice over a body of water. Remember to have available a rope or ladder in case of an emergency.

How to Make an Outdoor Rink

If no natural body of water is available, you can easily make a backyard rink. The base of the rink is made by packing down a level piece of ground and covering it with parallel sheets of sturdy polyethylene plastic that meet at the edges. Rim the circumference of the area with boards about six inches high, held in place with wooden stakes. If there is snow on the ground, a low dam of snow can be used to frame the rink.

When the air temperature is less than about 30° Fahrenheit (slightly below 0° Celsius), you can prepare the ice surface. This is done by using a garden hose and fine-spray nozzle to cover the entire rink surface with a thin layer of water. At the proper temperature, the water will quickly turn to ice, insulating and protecting the ice that will be laid down next. Once a fine layer of ice has been produced over the entire rink surface, the ice-making process goes faster. You can then flood the rink to a level of one to two inches. When this layer of ice is frozen solid, you're ready to skate. At the proper temperature, the whole process can be done overnight.

After you skate on the ice awhile, the surface becomes irregular. Smooth, fresh ice is more desirable for most skating, so you will want to resurface your ice. To do this, make sure first to remove all surface snow and ice from the rink with a broad shovel. Next, use the fine spray briefly again to fill in the cracks. Very little water will be necessary. (The sides of the rink were set at about six inches to allow for the buildup of ice with occasional respraying of the surface throughout the season.)

The seemingly impossible feat of skating outdoors in July is enjoyed by these skaters in Sun Valley, Idaho. Special equipment makes it possible to maintain skating ice even in summer.

Equipment

Skating is basically a matter of using skates on ice. Your skates relate you to the ice, so it is important that they be of good quality. A skate consists of two main parts: 1) the boot (the leather part that looks like a high-top shoe) combined with 2) the blade (the metal runner on which the actual skating is done).

Different types of skates are used for different kinds of skating. Perhaps the most readily available skate is the figure skate. It has a high boot attached to a blade that is suited for figure skating. The hockey skate has boots of stronger construction, to provide protection against injuries from stick and blade. Hockey boots tend to be cut somewhat lower in front than figure-skating boots. Hockey blades differ, too.

The figure-skating blade is broader and longer than its hockey counterpart and has a slight rockerlike curvature. No such curve appears in a hockey blade. There is one other difference in the blades—a most important one. The figure skate is not only somewhat broader but also has a concavity ground into the blade (see diagram). This concavity provides two edges for skating.

The hockey blade is rather flat-ground but narrower, and the skating is done on the entire width of the hockey blade rather than on edges.

Incidentally, speed skates are also available. They have boots that are softer and lower and blades that are longer, flatter, and narrower than those of either hockey or figure skates.

The differences in skate design are quite intentional and important. The more blade surface that comes into contact with the ice, the greater the speed that can be attained. The less the blade contact, however, the greater the maneuverability. So speed skates

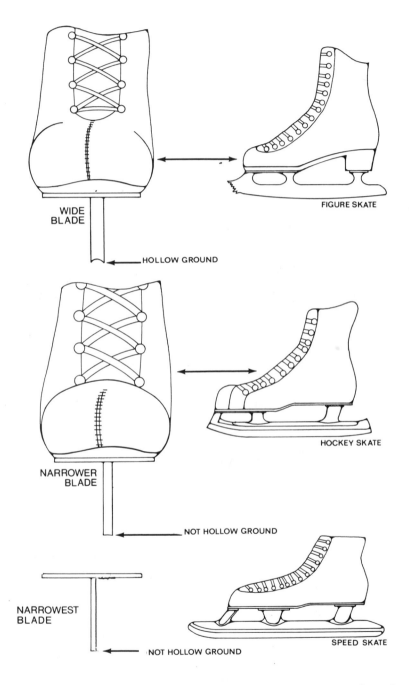

WIDE
BLADE

HOLLOW GROUND

FIGURE SKATE

NARROWER
BLADE

NOT HOLLOW GROUND

HOCKEY SKATE

NARROWEST
BLADE

NOT HOLLOW GROUND

SPEED SKATE

Each type of skate is designed to be more effective in the special use that is demanded of it. Credit: Diane A. Nolan.

are long and flat to provide utmost contact and speed. Figure skates are broader, and the gentle rockerlike arc limits the length of blade that is in contact with the ice at any time. Actually, figure skaters make contact with the ice on as little as a two-inch length of blade at a time. This gives great maneuverability.

An important element of the figure-skating blade is the toe pick. It is used by advanced skaters for some jumps and as a control factor in spinning; it is not used to propel the skater across the ice. Some beginning skaters actually remove the toe pick by grinding. This alteration is not recommended, since it disturbs the total balance of the skate.

Hockey skates fall midway in design between speed skates and figure skates. They are designed to have more blade contact than figure skates, and are therefore faster than figure skates. But hockey skates are shorter and therefore slower than speed skates.

Which skates are best for the beginning skater? Because of their stability and maneuverability, figure skates are recommended for all beginning skaters. The figure-skate blade gives the beginning skater a better feel of controlled relationship to the ice. The broader, more maneuverable figure blades and closer-fitting boots give the beginning skater a sense of security that he cannot enjoy at first in other types of skates. For this reason, most rental skates are of the figure-skating type.

Renting equipment at first is a good idea for new skaters. If your rink has good-quality, well-maintained rental equipment, you will be well advised to rent skates in the beginning. Renting offers several advantages over buying. First, rental skates are usually well broken in. The new skater has enough to do in learning to skate without the added problem of breaking in new skates. New boots, being somewhat stiff, take away some of the sense of contact with the ice that the new skater should try to develop. The other problem with new skating boots is much the same as with new shoes: sometimes your feet hurt from breaking them in.

Prevention of sore feet is one reason to make sure that skates, either rented or bought, fit properly. But it is not the most important reason. More important by far is the fact that properly fitting skates help to impart a feel of motion on the ice and support the foot and ankle, which provide security during that motion. Ill-fitting skates, either too tight or too loose, can be a catastrophe. Imagine the sensation of the new skater as feet go one way and loose-fitting skates go another!

Since it is of the utmost importance that skates fit properly, they cannot be bought this year with an eye toward the future. Skates to be worn this year must fit this year. There is nothing so frustrating to the new skater, particularly the child, as trying to learn to skate with boots that are sized for next year. Don't buy equipment for a child with a view to next season's use. If oversize boots cause this season not to go well, there may not be a next season.

Hand-me-downs offer the same problem of fit. They are usually stretched out of shape and ill-fitting. Hand-me-downs should be considered for use only if they really fit and have been properly reconditioned to work almost as well as new.

Good skates are fairly expensive. A skating boot is stronger than a street shoe and contains much more leather. Furthermore, blades come with the boots, an additional cost not often considered. So it is usual for skating equipment of adequate quality to be more expensive than a pair of comparable walking shoes. This is another reason skate rental may be a good idea for the beginner, at least at first.

What to Look for in Boots and Blades

Figure-skating boots should be made of top-grade leather throughout, with two layers of leather in the uppers. There should be a "counter" built in to support the ankle, running under the entire instep to support the arch as well. Look for a padded boot tongue that will protect the foot from being chafed by the laces. The sole should be of solid leather and should be capable of holding the screws or rivets that attach the blades. The heel should be made of layered leather nailed together from both inside the boot and outside.

These are the basic points to look for in a hockey boot as well. In addition, the hockey boot needs a protective toe box, like those found in safety shoes, to prevent injury. In recent years, hockey skates have been built high behind the foot to protect the Achilles tendon from injury.

Blades should be of high-quality tempered steel. Even the best blades will become dull with usage and require sharpening. Only good-quality blades can be successfully sharpened for prolonged use. Good-quality blades usually come with a shiny protective plating of nickel or chrome. Avoid blades with a dull finish; these usually will not sharpen well.

Fitting the Boot

Try your boots on with the socks you intend to wear for skating. Only one layer of sock is needed, preferably wool or cotton—the modern synthetic fibers tend to stretch and slip, sometimes causing chafing. You can expect your boot size to be one or one-and-a-half full sizes smaller than your regular shoe size. This is because a skating boot can fit more snugly than a walking shoe, since the toes do not flex as much in skating as in walking.

Do not expect a skating boot to feel as soft and comfortable as your street shoes.The boots are made firmer and sturdier to support the foot and ankle in motion. The boot should feel comfortably snug beneath the arch and around the ankle for good support.The counter should cup the heel and hold it firmly. A correctly fitted boot has a counter that ends just behind the ball of the foot, at the base of the big toe.

To be sure that the boots are properly fitted and laced (see page 15), and to seat your foot comfortably in the boot, walk around a bit on the floor before attempting to skate. Be sure to wear skate guards over your blades while doing this. (Skate guards, sheaths made of wood, plastic, or rubber, fasten to the blades and serve two purposes: 1) they prevent the blades from being dulled and 2) they prevent the blades from making marks on flooring. Skate guards are relatively inexpensive and reduce wear and tear on your blades when you are going to and from the ice.) Walk around in your skates until you feel comfortable.

Remember: if you can walk in your skates, you can skate in them. So let's walk over to the rink and begin.

How to Try on Your Skates

While the fit of the boot is important, your adjustment of the boot to the foot is even more so. As with ski boots, skating boots can be fitted closely to the foot by their fasteners. Ski boots are fastened with a series of clips or sometimes laces. Skating boots are always fastened with laces. The adjustment of the skating boot to the foot by use of the laces is critical. Small changes in the lacing pattern can considerably change the distribution of the body weight in the skate and against the blade, so it is important that the boot be laced properly.

Lacing boots is easy if you follow a few simple steps. It is important that you repeat these steps each time you put on your boots. In this way, you will have a constant relationship between your foot and your boot and a resulting consistency in how the ice feels when you skate.

Always sit down to put on skates. Choose a seat of comfortable height so that the skate blade rests as flat as possible on the floor. Do not attempt to lace your boots when only the toe or the heel of the blade is resting on the floor. Small children need a low seat to fasten their laces properly.

Once you are seated comfortably with the length of the blade resting on the floor, check the position of your foot and knee. When you lace your boot, make sure that your toes are pointed forward, aligned with your kneecap. Next, check to see that the weight of your leg is pushing down evenly over the blade. Now press your heel backward against the back of the skate. In this position, you are ready to lace your boots.

Lacing is easiest if the laces are put through the eyelets beforehand. Laces, incidentally, are made of either cotton or nylon. Cotton laces tend to grip a bit better and are less likely to stretch, but the nylon laces seem to last somewhat longer. Regardless of the type, laces grip better if you run them through the eyelets from outside the boot to inside.

Be sure that the laces are loosely threaded all the way from the toe before you start to tighten them. Be sure that your sock and boot tongue are pulled up and centered before you start to draw the laces tight. Now you are ready for the final step—drawing the laces tight.

Start tightening the laces from the bottom up. Pull the laces until the boot grips your foot firmly but not tightly. You should still be able to wriggle your toes, but you should not be able to slide your foot about inside the boot. Continue to draw the laces firm until you reach the point where your ankle bend occurs. Here you

Pull laces firmly up to this point.

Tie a simple overhand knot (half of a square knot).

tie the laces together in a simple overhand knot (half a square knot). At this point or a little above it, the eyelets give way to hooks.

Now raise the front of the blade off the floor so that the weight of your foot is cradled in the boot's heel. Don't forget to keep your toe, heel, and knee in line as before. Above the ankle it is not important that the laces be drawn quite so snugly, so lace a little less tightly from the boot crease to the top of the boot. Then tie the laces with a bow. It's a good idea then to tie the ends of the bow together with a common overhand knot to keep the knot secure. If there are long loose ends, tuck them into the boot top to keep them off the ice.

The properly laced boot fits snugly about the foot and ankle but is loose enough about the calf for you to easily slip one or two fingers between your leg and the boot. This space at the calf is necessary for free action of the calf muscles and the knee. Yet when you stand and walk in properly laced boots, there should be no movement of your heel inside the boot.

In new boots, wrinkles about the ankle are common. These may be a bit uncomfortable, but they will disappear as the boot breaks in. In a properly fitted boot, no more than one-and-one-half

Have heel seated as shown when you lace upper boot.

Leave enough room at top so you can tuck in lace ends.

inches of the boot tongue should be visible above the boot. If more than this is visible, the boots are too large.

New boots can be painful. A sore spot can be relieved by placing a soft, small facial sponge under the sock to protect the irritated area. Many skate shops have tools to mold leather and correct spot-fitting problems. As you can see, there are a great many variables to fitting a boot to a foot.

Most of the variables can be kept to a minimum by proper fitting. Final adjustment of boots is made by proper lacing. So it is essential that you do the lacing the same way each time.

Skating Lessons

In skating, as in everything else, nothing succeeds like success — so make things easy for yourself. Try to find a time when the weather conditions are comfortable and the rink is not too crowded, a time when you are ready for a pleasant new sensation unlike anything you have experienced before.

Skating is easy and fun, but there are a few basic things you will have to remember. The first basic is this: if you have skate guards, you will have to take them off before you step onto the ice.

Getting onto the Ice

Getting onto the ice is easy but requires a little knack. Hold the barrier with your right hand and sidestep onto the ice, your left

Peter Dunfield demonstrates how to sidestep onto ice.

17

foot first. This move will put you on the ice facing in the skating direction of most rinks, which is counterclockwise.

While you are still holding on to the barrier, alternately lift each foot up and down carefully in place. When you are comfortable with this action, let go of the barrier. You will find that you can stand on skates just about as easily as you can stand on your own two feet.

Next, raise your arms to what will be the skating position. Arms should be held at about waist level, just a bit in front of your body and with palms down. You use your arms to maintain balance in much the same way as a tightwire walker uses a pole.

In the ready position, arms are out and knees slightly bent.

Baby Steps

With your arms still in position and your feet slightly apart in normal standing position, bend your knees slightly and again lift your feet in place alternately. Toe out slightly. With your knees still slightly bent and your arms in the proper position, try six baby steps forward, turning your toes out just a bit as you do so. Turning your toes out helps you to walk on the ice. Repeat the series of six baby steps several times until you feel at ease doing it.

18

Lifting the left foot.   *Lifting the right foot.*

Gliding on Two Feet

    Now, using your six baby steps to get started, keep both feet on the ice, toes pointed forward, and you will find yourself gliding. When you glide, keep your feet parallel and aimed forward and

Correct: balance on upright blades.   *Wrong: Don't bend ankle and angle blade.*

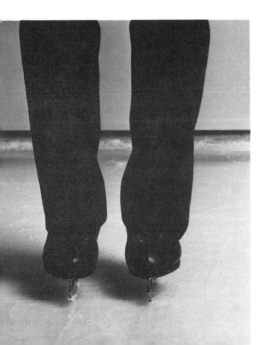

keep your weight evenly distributed on both feet. It is important to keep the blade in a perfectly upright position. A slight slant of either blade will make gliding more difficult.

The Dip

When you can glide comfortably, you are ready for the next maneuver, which is called the dip. The dip is a deep knee bend while gliding. To do the dip, move your arms from their position almost at your sides to a position directly in front of you. Then your arms will serve as a balance as you dip.

Here's how you do the dip.

To dip while gliding, extend both arms before you, hold your head up and your back straight, and bend your knees straight forward as much as you can without letting your ankles flop in or out. You will find yourself in a sitting position while gliding across the ice.

Falling

Now you are ready to take your first fall on the ice. From the dip position, allow your body to fall sideways. Resist the urge to use your hands and arms to break your fall. Instead, merely roll over on your thigh and hip. There! You're down on the ice after your

Oops! It can happen to anybody.   *Proper way to land is on your side.*

first fall. That wasn't as as bad as you thought it would be. As you learn to skate you'll fall occasionally. It won't hurt if you are relaxed and fall as you've learned to do here.

Falling from a standing position may prove a little more challenging, but it should cause you no greater discomfort. It is important to learn how to fall properly. Never try to break a fall with your hands and arms — that could result in a broken bone. If a fall seems unavoidable, allow your knees to drop into the dip position and then roll over as you have just done.

Standing After a Fall

To get up after a fall, roll over until you are on your hands and knees. Then raise one foot at a time to place the blades on the ice.

First move in getting up is to get onto hands and knees.

Then you get one foot up.

And next the other foot is up.

From that position (both your hands and feet are on the ice), stand up slowly.

Made it! Up again.

Lean

So far you have learned to glide forward with your skates and your body in a perfectly vertical position, which takes you in a straight line. To curve, it will be necessary for you to lean a bit away from the vertical.

While you are gliding comfortably straight ahead with your knees slightly bent and your feet comfortably apart, begin to lean by inclining both blades slightly to one side. This movement should be accompanied by a slight lean of your entire body to the same side. This combined action will curve your glide to the side of the lean.

Sonya Klopfer Dunfield demonstrates how to lean in a straight line from head to blade.

Now try leaning to the other side. When you can lean comfortably to both sides in a slow glide, try gliding a bit faster before starting to lean. The steeper the lean, the sharper the curve. Remember: lean from the blades up.

One-Foot Glide Forward

Now you are ready to try a one-foot glide. Begin by gliding on two feet. Gradually shift most of your weight onto the left foot. Then, by lifting your right knee, lift your right foot about six inches off the ice. Glide forward on the left foot for a few yards.

On one-foot forward glide, keep blade perpendicular to ice.

Then lower your right foot to the ice and do the exercise on the other side, removing your left foot from the ice and gliding on your right foot.

Next try the one-foot glide on a curve. To do this, begin with a two-foot glide. Lean to your left, inclining both blades to that side a bit. Now remove your right skate from the ice as you did in going from the straight-ahead two-foot glide to the one-foot glide. You will find that you continue to skate on one foot in a gentle arc to the left. The arc is caused by the construction of the figure skate. In this body position, you are skating on the outside edge of your left blade.

Now do this exercise on the right foot. You will find yourself skating on the outside edge of your right skate, arcing gently to the right.

24

One-foot glide on curve (using left outside edge).

Gliding on left outside edge and carrying free leg behind.

It is also possible to skate on the inside edges of your skates. Again beginning in a two-foot glide, lean gently to the left, inclining both skates to the left. This time, however, put most of your

One-foot glide on curve (using right inside edge).

Gliding on right inside edge and carrying free leg behind.

weight on your right skate. You will now find that you are skating on the inside edge of your right blade in a gentle arc toward the left.

Now try this maneuver to the other side. You will be skating on your left inside edge, arcing gently to the right.

First Movement Backward

Something about the word "back" upsets beginners in every sport. In tennis, for example, the word "backhand" itself seems to discourage beginners. This is true even though many tennis professionals emphasize the backhand as a normal swing, perhaps more normal than the forehand. Some people have hang-ups about backing a car down a driveway but have no hesitancy at all about driving forward.

So it is in skating. The simple suggestion of skating backward is enough to discourage many beginners. As in the examples just mentioned, there is no basis in fact for their fear.

The truth is that in certain respects skating backward is easier for the beginner than skating forward. The natural tendency of the beginner to look down toward his feet and the ice is somewhat of a help to backward movement, as looking down tends to place the weight of the body over the balls of the feet. When you skate forward, the same downward glance tends to inhibit good skating. Your weight should be toward the heels of your feet as you skate forward.

Backward Teeter-totter

Begin this movement by standing on the ice with the barrier directly in front of you. Grasp the barrier lightly but firmly with both hands. Be sure that your knees are very slightly bent, that your weight is equally distributed on both skates, and that your feet are comfortably apart. Rock gently to one side until the skate on the opposite side leaves the ice. Then rock in the opposite direction, planting the other skate on the ice and rocking gently until the first skate just barely leaves the ice. Practice rocking from one skate to the other, still holding on to the barrier, until you are comfortable with this motion. You have now learned half of what you need to do in order to skate backward.

At the start, weight is distributed equally on both feet.

Again standing motionless before the barrier and holding it lightly with both hands, try turning the toes of your skates in toward each other. You will find that the heels of the skates tend to drift outward a bit. You may also find that your ankles tend to fall in toward each other. This ankle turn-in is called "pronation." It is the normal position of the ankles for skating backward. Pronation is a normal and natural result of turning the toes inward. It is this position that has given rise to the term "weak ankles," although it is

Here's the rock left.

And here's the rock right.

a normal position. If your ankles pronate a bit when you are learning to skate backward, the movement will be easier to master. Practice turning your toes in and pronating your ankles until you are comfortable doing it.

Now put together the two movements: 1) the rocking and 2) the ankle pronation. With your toes pointed in and your ankles pronated, rock gently from side to side as you did before. You have only to let go of the barrier to begin skating backward.

To skate backward in a straight line, guide yourself by keeping a constant distance from the barrier. Or perhaps choose one of the blue or red lines painted under the ice (for hockey games) as a guide. It is best at first to skate backward along the shorter course at the end of the rink, rather than beginning at one of the long sides. The shorter sides have less traffic because they are not near the entrances to the ice.

By this time you have learned the basics of skating forward and backward. Practice will improve your confidence, technique, and ability.

You have also learned several things besides forward and backward motion. For example, you have learned to balance your weight on your skates while standing, bending, leaning, turning your toes inward, pronating, and rocking. All of this has taught you to transfer your weight from one skate to the other.

There is yet another principle of skating to which you have been introduced: the use of the edges of the blade in skating. As you skate backward in the teeter-totter with your weight thrust toward

When you skate forward, your weight rides at back of blade.   *When you skate backward, your weight rides under ball of foot.*

the inside of your boot, your weight is carried by the inside edge of the blade. In the two-foot lean, the weight is carried on the outside edge of the blade on the side to which you are leaning, and the inside edge of the blade on the other skate. So this is a good time to discuss the blade edges.

Edges

Remember that we selected figure skates for beginners because of their stability and maneuverability. These qualities are based on the structure of the skate. Look at your blade closely. Note the slightly arched trough that runs the length of the blade, leaving not one but two sharp edges for skating. You can actually fit the edge of a coin into the trough and slide it the length of the blade.

Skating on figure skates is done on one edge of the blade or the other. The same is true in using hockey skates, but hockey blades are narrower and have much less trough between the edges than figure skates.

To demonstrate edges to yourself, stand with your weight equally distributed on both skates placed parallel. Then incline your ankles toward each other (that is, toward the midline of your body). This action puts the weight on the inside edge of each skate.

Now try the opposite maneuver. Allow your ankles to incline away from each other, thrusting your weight to the outside edge of both skates. Remember that these ankle exercises are only to familiarize you with the edges. In actual skating, directing the weight to one edge or the other is done by total body lean to the desired side.

So you learned much more from skating backward than just the motion itself. You also learned about transfer of weight, and edging.

Two Gliding Exercises

And now we have two helpful gliding exercises: 1) the scooter push and 2) the swizzle.

Scooter Push

This is an exercise designed to improve your ability to push against the ice while gliding in balance. The motion is similar to

Starting position.   *Left foot turns out.*

Left foot thrusts from side of blade.

Pushing foot is lifted to side and behind skating foot.

the one used in riding a scooter, or nowadays a skateboard. You use your left foot as a scooter and learn to push with your right skate.

Stand in the basic starting position, feet parallel and comfortably apart, knees slightly bent, arms at waist level and a bit in front of your body with palms down. Now shift most of your weight onto your right skate so that you can feel it under the arch of your foot. Then pivot your left foot from the heel so that the toe points outward, making an angle of at least 45 degrees to the right skate. Using the inside edge of your left blade, press against the ice so that your body weight is propelled forward on the right skate. As your right skate glides forward, lift your left skate a little above the ice to a side position behind your right leg.

Now bring the left skate back beside the right skate and repeat the stroking maneuver. Using only your right skate for support and gliding, move all the way across the ice with the scooter push.

Then repeat the procedure, but this time glide on your left foot and push with your right. Practice this exercise until you are comfortable gliding on each foot and have mastered using the blade's edge, rather than the toe, for thrust.

The Swizzle

This is an exercise designed to improve your ability to use the inside edges of your blades as well as to improve your knee action. It is sometimes called "sculling" or "the grapevine" because of the vinelike pattern the skates trace on the ice.

To move forward in the swizzle from the basic starting position, turn your toes apart slightly, letting your weight fall on the inside edges. Press your skates evenly apart. This action will cause your body to move forward and your legs to go farther apart. Before the separation of your legs becomes uncomfortable, turn your toes inward again and draw your skates together.

To start swizzle, turn your toes apart on inside edges.

Then push your feet apart.

You will find that as your feet go apart, your knees bend a bit more than they do in the starting position. As you draw your legs together again, your knees straighten again and your body rises a bit. The development of knee action begins with this gentle falling

Feet are this far apart at widest separation.

of the body with bending of the knees as the feet go apart and rising of the body as the knees straighten again in drawing the feet together.

The same exercise should be done in a backward direction. This time, point your heels out to begin the motion. Then point them back together again to complete it. By the time you have reached this stage in your progress, you should be able to skate forward and backward with ease and confidence. It is about time to stop.

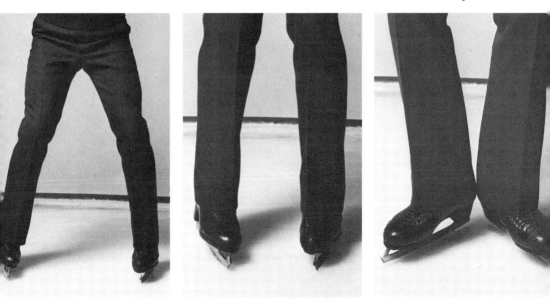

Then turn toes in. *Draw feet together.* *Turn toes out, and begin again.*

Stopping on Skates

There are several ways to stop. The most common ones are: 1) the snowplow stop, 2) the T stop, and 3) the hockey stop. The snowplow stop is based on the swizzle exercise you have just been practicing. Beware: sharp blades make learning to stop most difficult.

Snowplow Stop

From a gliding position on both skates, turn your heels out, using the inside edges of both blades under the arch to shave the

Blade of proper sharpness allows you to shave ice on inside edge.

ice. Be sure to keep your weight equally distributed on both feet. Allow your knees to flex gently to absorb the energy of the stop. Very sharp blades will catch in the ice rather than shave it, and therefore make correct stopping impossible.

In the snowplow, you use inside edges of both skates under the arch to shave ice.

T Stop

The T stop also uses the blade edge to stop motion. In the T stop, however, it is the *outside* edge of one skate that does the work. To use the T stop, you must first learn the T position.

This is done first with use of the barrier for balance. Start by facing the barrier in the usual starting position, resting your hands lightly on the barrier for balance. Raise your left foot and place it behind the heel of the right boot with your left instep at your right heel. This position of the skates is known as the T position.

Now raise your left foot from the ice and move it to a position about six inches behind your right heel. Then incline your left blade so that the *outside* edge of the left blade beneath the arch comes in contact with the ice. Then draw your left foot toward the

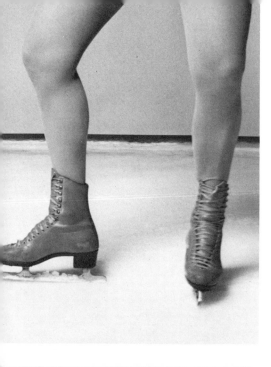

To do a T stop, begin shaving ice well behind skating foot (above left). Drawing the shaving edge to the heel of the skating foot (above right). Stopped (left).

right heel, using the left outside edge to shave the ice. Repeat this exercise until the action is smooth and consistent, and then practice stopping with the other foot.

Now move away from the barrier, using the scooter push to begin your motion. Position the pushing foot in a T position behind the gliding foot. Gently lower the blade until its outside edge comes into contact with the ice about six inches behind the skating blade. Then gradually draw the braking foot toward the heel of the skating foot, using the outside edge to shave the ice gently. With practice, you will also learn to gradually shift your weight from the gliding foot to the braking foot as you stop. You may have a tendency to turn during the T stop, but this can be overcome. When braking with your left foot, reach forward with your right arm as if to open a door.

Also practice the T stop using your right foot for braking. Practice so that you become equally proficient with both feet.

Hockey Stop

The hockey stop uses a combination of snowplow-stop and T-stop techniques. Start with a two-foot glide forward, your arms and shoulders facing in the skating direction. As you glide, twist

Hockey stop shaves ice with both blades, as shown.

37

your hips quickly to the left (right hip forward), at the same time bending your knees a bit and using the left blade's outside edge and the right blade's inside edge to shave the ice. This maneuver should be done gently at first, using both feet to shave the ice smoothly.

· With practice, the hockey stop can become the most effective means of stopping quickly. Especially when you are going fast, the hockey stop can be quite thrilling, often sending a shower of shaved ice through the air for several feet in front of you.

By this time, you should feel comfortable skating forward, skating backward, and stopping. This means that you can travel on the ice with confidence. You have been able to come to a stop and take off again in a new direction. Possibly you have already found some other ways of changing direction while moving. Let's explain some of the possibilities.

Turns

•

In turning, the position and movement of your arms becomes more important. Remember that in the T stop you use the opening-the-door position of your arm in order to stabilize the braking action. In the hockey stop, you use your arms to stabilize the twisting action of your hips. In the turns, you will make further use of your arms, your hips, and the reaction between the two in order to assist the turning action.

Unweighting Your Skates

Turns are easier if some of the weight of your body is lifted off the blade at the time of the turn. You achieve the "unweighting" by using your knees in either a rising or a falling motion. To understand this effect, stand on your bathroom scale and note your weight. Then bend your knees suddenly and allow your body to sink toward the ground. Note that the scale dial suddenly reads several pounds less. In allowing your weight to sink toward the ground, you have momentarily relieved the amount of pressure exerted on the scale. The other way to produce unweighting is to start in a crouch position and straighten your knees suddenly to rise a bit. For an instant the scale will read more than your normal weight, but in another moment it will briefly read less than normal. This motion, too, demonstrates unweighting.

Unweighting of skates makes any turning action in skating easier. (Incidentally, this principle holds true for skiing, too.)

Two-Foot Turn

Begin by moving in the forward two-foot glide position, with your hands at waist level and slightly in front of you, as described previously. Now, with the index finger of your right hand, point in the direction you are moving. At the same time, use the index finger of your left hand to point in the direction from which you have come. Be sure that you are traveling in a straight line with your weight equally distributed on both feet. For this turn only, do

Gliding forward.

not incline your skates to either side. The turn is done by twisting your hips to the left so that your toes go through an arc of 180 degrees (a half circle) and then point in the same direction as your left hand. You are then gliding backward with your right arm still pointing in the direction of travel but your toes pointing in the opposite direction.

This two-foot turn will be facilitated somewhat if you use your knees to lift your body a bit at the same time as you perform the twisting motion.

As you did with the other exercises, practice the two-foot turn to

Twist hips left.   *Gliding backward.*

left and right, while moving forward and while moving backward. Understand that in these turns your body continues to move in its original direction, but the direction in which you face (from the hips down only) has changed. In skating, this change of facing is known as a turn. There are also changes of direction while you continue facing in the direction of motion at all times. These too are called turns, and are very similar to turns that you make on a bicycle.

Mohawk

The Mohawk turn is another change in facing while you continue along in the same direction of motion. To do a Mohawk, you change your facing while shifting your weight from one foot to another. This motion is similar to the open-hipped dancing position of the American Indians from whom it got its name.

The most important and easiest Mohawk turn for the beginner is the one that goes from the right inside edge while skating forward to the left inside edge skating backward. To do this, begin

41

Begin with one-foot forward glide on right inside edge.

the Mohawk from a one-foot forward glide on the right inside edge. Keep your right arm pointed in the direction of your movement. Your left leg is off the ice in a position extended behind your right heel and a bit to the side. Your left hand points in the direction you are moving away from.

While keeping your left blade off the ice, bring your left foot to a position in which the heel of the left blade is pointed at the arch of the right foot. Continue to skate on the right inside edge in a

Left skate is drawn to T-position, as shown.

Gliding backward on inside edge of left foot.

strong arc. Now simultaneously do three things: 1) twist your hips strongly to the left, 2) put your left blade on the ice, and 3) lift your right blade off the ice. This combination of moves will transfer your weight from your right skate moving forward to your left skate moving backward. It is important to maintain your motion in a continuous arc while doing a Mohawk turn.

This Mohawk turn can be done in either direction, so practice going from right foot to left foot and from left foot to right foot. There are many other kinds of Mohawk turns, each a change of facing accompanied by change of skating foot.

Gliding on inner forward edge.

Free heel is drawn to arch of gliding foot.

Rotate hips left, and change feet.

Glide away with free leg extended.

3 Turn

The 3 turn is a change of facing done on one foot. In the process of doing the 3 turn, your skate actually draws the numeral 3 on the ice.

Begin with a one-foot glide on the left outside edge (only the left

Start the 3 turn with forward glide on left outside edge. (Note the 3 pattern marked on ice.)

skate is in contact with the ice). As in the Mohawk turn, your right arm is pointing forward and your left arm is pointing in the direction from which you have come, twisting slightly at your waist to the left. Make sure that the toe of your right foot is carried about twelve inches behind your left heel.

To turn, release the twist in your waist. Twist your hips to the left and at the same time twist your arms to the right. As in the other turns, this motion will be simplified if you rise slightly by straightening your knees *as* you turn. At the completion of the turn, your right foot should still be in the same position relative to the skating foot. If the free right foot is carried too much to one side or the other of the skating heel, it will be difficult to maintain your balance. As with the other turns, this turn should also be practiced to the other side on the other foot.

There are numerous other kinds of 3 turns, many of which are much more difficult. So begin with this 3 turn, done on the left outside edge. Incidentally, it's easiest because most people skate

Twist shoulder against left hip.

Turning: release hips left under shoulders.

Continue twisting hips to left under shoulders.

counterclockwise at the rink, thereby developing strength in the left outer forward position.

Completed 3-turn position.

Diagram shows overhead view of skater doing a 3 turn. Credit: Diane A. Nolan.

 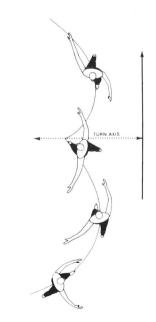

Forward Crossover

The last of the basic skating maneuvers you should learn well is the forward crossover. The crossover is a way of skating around a corner faster than by using a simple gliding turn. Crossovers will also help you to develop more power in your skating, so it is especially valuable for hockey players.

To learn the forward crossover, begin with a two-foot glide on a curve to the left. Remember that to do this, you must incline your blades a bit to the left and shift your weight in that direction, at the same time keeping your weight evenly distributed on both feet. Your weight will be on the outside edge of your left blade and the inside edge of your right one. Now, while gliding to the left in a

Stroke onto left outside forward edge.

gentle curve, shift your weight so that most of it rests on your left skate. Now bend your right knee gently, lifting your right foot off the ice about six inches. Pass your right skate in front of your left skate and place the right blade on the ice parallel to and across in front of the left blade.

This maneuver brings your legs into a crossed position, which is

Draw right leg around and forward.　　　*Right leg crosses over left.*

difficult to hold for more than a brief moment. As soon as the right skate meets the ice, you must transfer your weight to the right skate, carefully lifting your left skate off the ice at the same time. The result is a position in which your weight is resting completely on your right skate, using the right inner edge. Now

Weight shifts to right skate.　　　*Push with left skate, and then lift it.*

Return left skate to side-by-side start position.

bring the left skate around behind the right foot and up beside it, placing the left blade on the ice again so that you are once more in the two-foot glide position, curving gently to your left.

Practice this maneuver until you can do it easily, repeating the maneuver three or four times in succession. Then try the same type of motion to the right, bringing the left skate off the ice to crossover in front of the right skate, shifting your weight to the left skate, and bringing your right foot around and up beside the left one again.

Proper arm position is important for balance during the crossover. To prepare for crossovers, a specific arm position is necessary. Hold your arms at waist level, your forward arm slightly lower than the other. For crossovers to the left, your right arm should be held in front of the body, pointing in the direction in which you are going; the left arm should be held behind the body, pointing in the direction from which you have come. This point should be done while your shoulders are fairly square toward the direction of motion. Twist just a little at the waist so that your right shoulder is only slightly ahead of the left one. This position of arms and shoulders is important for maintaining balance, but too much twist of your shoulders or your waist may remove the necessary feel of lean from this maneuver.

Crossover Exercises

Two simple exercises will improve your crossovers.

The first one begins with an old friend, the scooter-push exercise. Get started by gliding on the left outside edge and then use the scooter push with the right foot, moving gently to the left on a curve. Remember to keep your skating knee constantly bent just a bit. Continue to push smoothly with your right leg, using the blade, not the toe, to push with. Remember to extend your right leg fully to the side and behind the left skate. This scooter-push exercise on a curve will help you achieve the balance on your left outside edge that is vital for doing crossovers. It will also smooth out your push action with the right leg. The exercise should be repeated gliding on the outside edge, pushing with the left skate.

The second exercise for improving your crossovers is called the scissors. To prepare for it, review the swizzle, which was done on a straight line. The scissor is a motion that allows your skates to draw a pattern that crosses and uncrosses on the ice without your removing either skate from contact with the ice at any time.

Start this exercise by doing two or three swizzle motions. As you complete a swizzle, allow your right foot to glide forward in front of the left one. As you do this, shift your weight from the inner

Begin as though doing a swizzle, pushing your feet apart.   *Draw your feet together.*

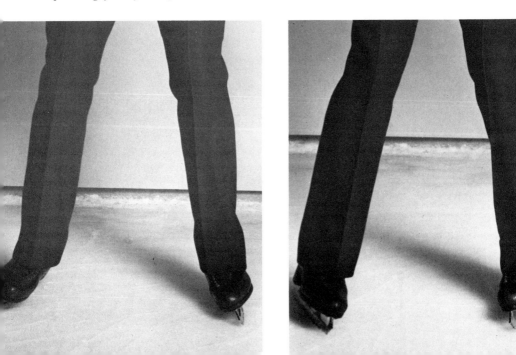

Cross your right skate in front.

edge of the left skate to the outer edge, thus moving your feet to the crossed position. Then, quickly (before your feet cross too far) direct your toes toward the midline to uncross your feet. In the uncrossed position, the left skate will again slip over to its inside edge.

This scissor exercise, of course, can be done crossing the other way. The exercise is designed to develop the strength of the back foot in the crossover. It has been described from a straight-line

Push your left skate behind your right.

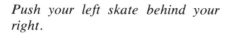

 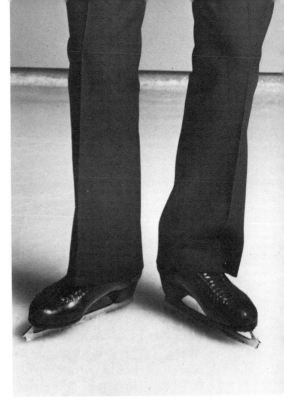

Uncross, on both blades on ice.   *Push apart to starting position.*

approach, beginning with the swizzle. To relate it more directly to crossovers, begin the exercise swizzling on a curve. Set the arms as they would be in a crossover.

Back Stroking

Back stroking is built from the basic teeter-totter motion. By being more precise with your foot positions and strengthening your knee action, you can develop a powerful backward stroke.

Begin in a backward teeter-totter as described on page 26. Make your motions more exacting as you shift your weight from one foot to the other, bringing your feet together after each stroke. Your knees should be flexed and close at each change of foot.

Thrust to the side from the inside front part of the pushing blade. Push about a foot to the side, but no more. A wider push

Back stroke onto left inside edge.

Transfer weight to right inside edge.

Turn head to look toward direction of motion.

Transfer weight to left skate again. Note: all changes of feet should be done when feet are close together before thrust.

will tend to shift your weight off your gliding foot and onto your pushing foot, destroying your backward flowing motion and balance. As you rise from the gliding knee, raise the thrusting foot off the ice to a position directly in front of the gliding foot. Draw your free leg straight back beside your skating (gliding) foot as you flex both knees into the ready position. Shift your weight to the new foot, repeat the process on the other foot.

As you do this, your free leg will pass through a triangular pattern. At first, backward motion will be on shallow, inside edges. As your motion accelerates and your rhythm improves, a stronger lean to the inside edge of your pushing foot will shift your weight to an outside-edge stroke.

The most serious error in backward stroking is putting too much force on your pushing foot and not retaining enough weight on your rising, skating knee and foot.

Forward Stroking

Forward stroking is one of the basic movements of figure skating. It is based on the motion you learned in the scooter-push exercise. Stand in the starting position and do a scooter-push with your right leg. Now, instead of returning the pushing right foot to the ice, extend the right leg behind you and beside you at a 45-degree angle. Hold the leg in that position while gliding smoothly on your left leg, knee slightly bent. Now return your right skate to a position beside your left skate on the ice. With both knees slightly bent, gradually transfer your weight to the right leg and thrust with the left leg and foot at this time. Stroke along the ice alternating left and right legs for skating.

Stroke onto right foot.

Feet come close together for change of feet.

Stroke onto left foot.

Feet again come close together for change of feet.

Skating Backward on a Two-Foot Curve

From the backward two-foot glide, pick up one foot as in the forward one-foot glide, and stroke backward for momentum. Next, glide on two feet; lean to one side, inclining your skates to the center of the arc. Concentrate on keeping the feet parallel, slightly to the inside edges. Alternately lift one foot and then the other while in the two-foot curve. Do this gliding backward in the other direction. Carry your free foot about twelve inches or less off the ice. This practice will begin to develop a motion that can eventually be used for backward crossovers and will train all your back skating motions on a curve.

Free-Skating Exercises

In most countries, special organized programs are provided to develop skaters from the earliest years. An effort is made to teach the basic skating skills to all skaters, regardless of whether they will go on to figure skating, hockey, or speed skating. It is considered important that all skaters develop basic competence in the use of their bodies and their skates before they specialize in the particular branch of skating that claims their interest. The following exercises will provide you with increased confidence in your ability to skate and improve your skating by reinforcing your skills. Frequent repetition of these exercises will also strengthen those parts of your body most used for each skating maneuver.

Two-Foot Spin

The two-foot spin is an exercise for better balance on ice. It is also one of the most exciting movements in skating. A spin is a rotation of the entire body over a center that is in a fixed position on the ice. In the two-foot spin, the center of the rotation is midway between your feet, which bears the weight of your body equally.

In a standing position, your arms extended and your trunk rotated to the right, place your left toe pick in the ice, about a foot ahead of your right skate in widespread T position. Keep most of your weight on your left toe, left knee slightly flexed. Now draw your arms a quarter turn to the left, stopping them in front of your body. At the same time, skate your right foot around the left in the same direction your arms are moving. As your rotation

58

begins, shift your weight off the left toe and let it rest evenly on both feet, using both inside edges just a bit. To add speed to your spin, draw your arms to a hand-clasp position in front of your chest. This is the first step toward developing a spinning motion. It may produce only three or four rotations. You may find this method of starting to spin too basic, so here is another approach to spinning.

Moving Start

Glide forward on two feet. Now shift your weight mostly to the left skate and turn that foot out. This action will cause your feet to separate. Skate your right foot around the left one, swinging your arms around to the left. When the spin starts, shift your weight until it is half on each foot, and draw your arms in and your legs together.

Spiral Position

The spiral position is one in which your weight is supported on one leg while your other leg is extended behind your body and in the line of motion. That free leg is in such a position that the foot and your head are on the same horizontal plane. Learning the

Page Polk demonstrates gliding with her free leg extended.

59

spiral position will help you more gracefully to develop balance and strength of your back and legs.

From a gliding motion on either foot, slowly extend your free leg behind the heel of your skating foot, raising your free leg as high as possible. Keep both arms at your sides for balance. Try to

Free leg is raised slowly.

keep your back arched, your neck and head held high without pushing your chin up. The gliding motion will make balancing easy.

Free leg is raised as high as possible and back is kept arched.

At some point you will be unable to raise your leg higher without lowering your trunk. So, using your hip joint as a swivel point, allow your upper body to move forward and downward as your free leg rises behind you to balance. Remember to lower your trunk at the hip joint, rather than using your neck and waist to lower your head.

Keep your arms extended to the side of your body for best balance throughout. Reaching forward to grasp for support may

Front view of the same spiral position.

thrust you forward onto the toe pick of the skate, which could result in a sudden stop and forward fall.

To come out of the spiral position, gently and slowly straighten upright.

Bunny Hop

The bunny hop is the basic stretched motion that skaters use to spring from the ice. It is the fundamental jump done from a forward edge and is the basis of forward edge jumps. The bunny hop is a coordination maneuver synchronizing the motion of your free leg, your jumping knee, and the rhythm of your arms.

To help you coordinate all the elements before actually jumping, here is an exercise. From a one-foot glide on your left foot,

Deborah Page demonstrates stroking to take-off for bunny hop.

with your knee slightly bent, swing your right leg directly forward from the hip. As you do this, rise on your skating knee, with your right skate directly in front of you and about a foot above the ice. Then, bending your skating knee, return your right skate back. As your right skate passes your left skate, push with the toe pick of your right skate. This movement synchronizes the rise and fall of the knee with the leg swing and introduces the landing motion using the toe pick of the free blade.

While you are doing this leg movement, your arms should swing freely in a natural but slightly exaggerated walking rhythm. When

Here's the swing and spring.

you can do this exercise smoothly, successively alternating the use of right and left legs for skating, you are ready to jump.

The bunny hop is a forward jump on a straight line without rotation. During the jump, your legs make a single scissor motion. The takeoff is from one foot, the landing on the other. Proper timing of your spring from the ice is essential. Start your spring into the air as your free foot begins its forward motion. You must be jumping just as your free leg, in its forward swing, passes your skating leg. Springing into the air too late may cause you to fall over backward.

Here is the whole bunny-hop motion. Stroke forward for momentum; left, right, left. As you start this third stroke, flex your left knee strongly and press into the ice to spring up. Coordinate the jumping motion with the swing of your free foot straight forward. Remember to synchronize your arm motion as you do in your regular walking rhythm. Keep your back straight throughout so that your head leads your body into the air. Keep your eyes

Reaching for air.

looking forward at all times. Looking down may tend to make you lean forward and fall forward. Landing is onto your right toe, then immediately onto the left foot glide. The toe landing acts as a cushion to the landing and feeds the motion forward onto the left foot glide.

Right-toe landing.

To glide on left foot.

Rink Rules and Courtesy

Ice rinks are busy places. Like other places where large numbers of people come together, rinks have certain rules and customs that tend to make the experience more enjoyable for everyone. The rules have been developed over the years to assure the comfort and safety of all the skaters. Before you go to a public rink, you should familiarize yourself with these rules. You will thereby save yourself the embarrassment and discomfort that sometimes befall newcomers to skating.

Rink managers generally set aside various hours for different types of skating. Beginners will probably start in the public sessions. There are also periods of time set aside for hockey players, and still other hours for figure skaters. Consult your rink director about the hours that apply to you.

Remember that most ice rinks charge an admission fee. There is also a fee for skate rental. Most rinks require that personal articles such as handbags, shoes, and heavy outer garments be checked. Smoking may be permitted in some areas, but never on the ice. Nor is eating or drinking on the ice permitted at well-run ice rinks. Pets are specifically excluded from the entire rink facility.

There is a special pattern of traffic flow in general skating sessions. The skaters move in a counterclockwise direction, usually using the area nearest the barrier for this purpose. Their route is called "the track." When you step onto or off the ice, be careful not to cut across the flow of traffic.

The center area of the rink is customarily used for teaching beginners how to skate. In some rinks, figure skaters use the center of the ice to practice specific movements. In other rinks, at a public session, plastic cones like those you see on highways may be used to set off a special area of the ice for skating instruction or figure skating during a less-busy public session. Cones are also used to mark off areas of the ice that are unsafe. In any event, cones placed on the ice are there for a purpose. If you have any doubt about what that purpose is, ask a rink attendant.

Rink attendants enforce skating rules and assist skaters in difficulty. Attendants can be called upon to enforce the rules of the rink if a skater is having difficulty because the rules are being broken. For example, playing tag on the ice is not allowed at most rink sessions. If you're having problems with skaters who are playing tag, feel free to call upon a rink guard for help. Call him also if you have an accident or injury, or if you see one. Do not confuse the rink guards with skating instructors. The rink guard is an attendant who may or may not be able to teach. Teaching at the rink is done by a qualified instructor.

Here is a list of do's and don'ts to help make your time on the ice more enjoyable.

Do skate with the traffic. If the traffic direction changes, change your direction with it. Don't try to skate against the traffic.

Do skate steadily in your chosen direction. Don't weave in and out among less-experienced skaters.

Don't skate while carrying an infant or small child. Do skate with your small child in the middle of the ice, away from the track.

Breaking the Ice

Skating is a social experience. It is as easy to make friends on the ice as anywhere else, and often easier. It is acceptable to skate up to another skater and talk about skating. Most beginners will relish tips from more-experienced skaters, and most experienced skaters enjoy sharing their knowledge. Beginners also like to talk to other skaters who are sharing or have already experienced their early challenge on the ice. As your skating improves, you may want to skate with someone else. Once you are comfortable on the ice yourself, it's permissible to offer to skate with someone else. But remember, pick someone who skates at your level or is willing to come down to it.

How to Dress

Dressing for skating is like dressing for anything else: prepare yourself for the conditions you expect to meet. You will not need to be dressed as warmly for skating indoors as for skating outside.

The air temperature at most indoor ice rinks is 50° to 60° year-round. You will feel quite comfortable in a blouse and sweater or thin jacket plus loose-fitting slacks, moderately cut. Slacks for men or women that are cut too tight inhibit proper leg movement, particularly knee bend. Slacks that are cut too loose, particularly at the cuffs, can be dangerous if the cuff drags on the ice and catches on the skate. Slacks have an advantage over skirts in that they protect the legs should a fall occur.

Most skaters wear gloves. The hands and feet are the radiators of the body, through which body heat escapes. If you can keep your hands and feet warm, your body temperature will remain stable. The feet are already covered by a pair of light socks and the skating boot. The hands should be covered by a pair of warm gloves that will conserve body heat and also provide protection from ice burn if you fall. Hats are not customarily worn indoors, but are often worn outdoors to conserve body heat.

For outdoor skating, the skater will want to be dressed a little more heavily. The same gloves may be useful, or perhaps heavier mittens. The feet will again be covered with light socks and skates, but for prolonged outdoor skating, boot covers are sometimes helpful. These can be made inexpensively from an old pair of heavy socks. Slit the sole of the sock down the middle from heel to toe. Before putting on your skates, pull each sock up the leg to just below the knee. Once the skates are on, slide the sock down to cover the boot. Use a safety pin or two under the boot to hold the two sides of the sock together and keep it in place.

Heavier clothing may also be required for your body. Here the key is layers of clothing. Several light, flexible layers of clothing are more suitable for skating than a single heavy parka. A turtleneck sweater is preferable to a scarf for neck warmth. Scarves tend to loosen and fall off with the motion of skating. A loose scarf can pose a hazard for the skater or people around him.

Over the turtleneck, a nylon shell top is very effective in sealing in body heat and keeping out cold and wind. A heavy sweater usually goes over this. The same slacks that are used for skating indoors are helpful outdoors, but they probably must be accompanied by thermal underwear or tights.

There are a few no-no's for skating attire, too. Do not wear a long scarf on the ice. Do not wear loose items of clothing or jewelry that can fall off and clutter the ice, producing a hazard for other skaters. Make sure that your hair is restrained so it does not interfere with your vision. If you wear glasses, use some device to keep them on your head, as you would for tennis or skiing.

There is, of course, no special clothing required for skating. The foregoing suggestions are for the skater's comfort and safety. Any clothing that is comfortable, safe, and warm is suitable. Girls do not need a figure-skating costume such as they might see on television. Boys do not need the special sweater, uniform, or equipment that the hockey player uses. In fact, hockey sticks are specifically prohibited from the ice during general skating sessions.

For skating indoors or out, dress comfortably, warmly, and sensibly.

Skating Organizations

Over the years, ice skating has become an organized recreation. Several organizations promote and direct activities in the sport.

One of the oldest and most highly respected organizations in American amateur sports is the United States Figure Skating Association. It is the governing body of amateur figure skating in the United States. Through its member clubs, the USFSA sponsors the competitions that lead to national and international championships in figure skating, including singles, pairs, and dance. The USFSA also directs a nationally accepted testing program, which takes the skater from basic skills to the highest levels of proficiency in figure skating, free skating, pair skating, and dancing. The organization provides many publications of interest to the skater, and a number of excellent films. The address of the United States Figure Skating Association is: 178 Tremont Street, Boston, Massachusetts 02111.

Another important organization in skating is the Ice Skating Institute of America. This group includes people who manage rinks, skating-school directors, and skating instructors. It also numbers among its members people who build ice rinks and supply them, and people who sell ice-skating equipment and clothing. The ISIA works to set industry standards for recreational skating, and sponsors a testing program that has been highly successful in introducing the basic skills of skating to large numbers of recreational skaters. The ISIA also has some publications of interest to skaters. Their address is: 1000 Skokie Boulevard, Wilmette, Illinois 60091.

The professionals who teach the basic skills of all skating and the advanced techniques in figure skating belong to the Professional Skaters Guild of America. This group administers a certification and rating system for professional instructors that is based on a highly refined structure of tests for the instructor. The Guild offers some publications of general interest to the recreational skater and figure skater. Their address is: P.O. Box 80, Elma, New York 14059.

Skater's Energy Diet

Man does not skate on bread alone. Fad diets to the contrary, the skater, like all other athletes, needs a well-balanced diet complete with proteins, fats, carbohydrates, and all the necessary vitamins and minerals. This may not be news to professional athletes, whose training tables are often carefully supervised, but to participants in the solo sports like skating and tennis, proper diet may be a new concept.

For example, a few years ago a physiologist named Ostrand suggested that a diet high in carbohydrate might increase endurance. He did some work with animals which seemed to show that he was on to something. So in Europe, and in America too, some athletes have come to train between competitions with a diet high in protein to "build muscles" but then switch to a high-carbohydrate diet a week before the big event. "Carbohydrate loading" of this type, done just before competition to increase endurance, has not been particularly helpful.

But there is some truth to the concept that carbohydrates are needed for action. The body burns carbohydrate foods such as bread, potatoes, cake, noodles, and sugars to supply energy. For the average boy or girl, getting through a usual day may require some 2,200 to 3,400 calories. Smaller kids use less, larger or older ones more, and as a rule boys burn more calories than girls. But active sports such as free skating may require as much as 1,800 calories each hour for energy. Patching (practicing school figures on a patch of ice) is less strenuous and burns fewer calories. But even on patch, a certain number of extra calories are used to keep the body temperature normal in the chilly rink.

How can you tell if your calorie intake is enough? The answer is

Active sports such as free skating (the split jump shown here is not for beginners) may burn up as much as 1,800 calories each hour.

quite simple: if you have enough energy and are neither gaining nor losing weight, you are eating the right amount of calories. To find out how many this is, get a calorie-counter booklet, the kind sold in most drugstores. For a day or two, jot down everything you eat, including the amounts. Look up the number of calories contained in each serving and add them up. That will give you a rough idea of how many calories you are taking in in a day. If your weight stays constant, your calorie intake is probably adequate.

As you will note from using your calorie counter, other foods besides carbohydrates also contain usable calories. Proteins and fats are good sources of calories. Your diet will, of course, include some of these. When using the calorie counter, remember to list everything you eat. You will probably be surprised at the large number of calories you are taking in. Take the case of a skater we know well, a fourteen-year-old girl named Page who weighs about ninety-five pounds. In a usual school day without skating, she may use about 2,500 calories, but for each hour of free skating, she needs about 1,000 calories extra. So two hours of free style will add about 2,000 calories, for a total of 4,500 calories on a busy, hard-working day. That is why, although she eats like a man twice her size, her weight stays at ninety-five pounds. And that's why you hardly ever see a chubby competitive skater.

The calories are only the beginning, not the end, of the dietary needs. To burn calories, vitamins are needed, particularly the B vitamins. So with the increased need for calories comes a need for extra vitamins. In a properly arranged diet full of fresh leafy green vegetables, whole-grain cereals, and lean red meats, enough vitamins would be supplied automatically. But in this era of highly processed and refined foods, sometimes the calories come without the needed vitamins. It is possible to see signs of B-vitamin deficiency in skaters whose calorie intake exceeds their vitamin intake. Such signs include cracks at the corners of the mouth, smooth tongue, hand tremor, and skin rash. These patients may complain of nervousness, sleeplessness, irritability, and easy fatiguing. Treatment for the vitamin deficiency is simple: extra B vitamins. Since B vitamins are not stored in the body and therefore can't be taken to excess, it might be a good idea for some skaters to take extra B vitamins when they are training hard.

Most skaters in their growing years would normally build muscle with the foods that bring protein into the body. Skating may add even more muscle, so they need more protein-containing foods. Such foods include meats, fish, eggs, poultry, milk and cheese, peas and beans and nuts. Protein foods tend to be more expensive than the carbohydrate ones, and usually are not readily available at the rink snack bar. To assure yourself of enough protein, take your meals at home as often as possible.

The growing body needs such minerals as calcium to build bones and iron to build blood. These are usually present in large-enough quantity in diets that have sufficient amounts of protein foods. Unlike B vitamins, calcium and iron can cause trouble if taken in too-large amounts, so these minerals, as well as vitamins A and D, should be used only under a doctor's direction. What of the idea of vitamin E for strength or vitamin C for endurance? So far as is known, there is no benefit to be gained by the skater from taking extra vitamins of any kind, except the B vitamins we just mentioned.

But it may be a good idea, particularly in warm weather, to take in extra fluid and perhaps a little extra salt. Sweating takes both salt and water out of the body at a rapid rate. Symptoms of lack of salt and water include tiredness, headache, nausea, and especially muscle cramps. So drink adequately, and in warm weather perhaps use a little extra salt. As a rule, it is hard to take in too much water, so drink it freely. You know you're taking enough when you feel the urge to put some of it out again every few hours. If you go from morning to night without that urge, you're probably not drinking enough water.

It is possible for a hundred-pound skater to lose as much as three pounds of fluid through sweating in an hour or so of vigorous work. Since a quart of water weighs about two pounds, it will take about a quart-and-a-half of water to replace the amount lost from an hour of hard work. The amount of salt that is lost varies with the season and with the condition of the skater, so there is no good way to approximate the amount to be replaced. Gatorade is a liquid designed to replace salt and water in the proportions in which it is lost. Gatorade is used by many teams for fluid replacement, but it is a rather expensive way to buy salt and water.

Is it important for the skater to make changes in his or her food habits just before a competition? Most athletes have learned not to eat for four to six hours before a contest; some of them do not eat for as long as twelve hours. Skating is as violent an exercise as any other, to say nothing of the dizzying jumps and spins, so you would certainly do well to avoid eating within a few hours of competition. It is not, however, a good idea to go too long without fluids. Keep drinking clear liquids such as water and fruit juice until about an hour before competition.

In any event, proper diet is essential to proper training for the skater. Between competitions and during competitions, you will probably skate as well as you eat.

Stretch Exercises

Watch out, skaters! The football players are catching up to you. In the past few years, several pro football teams have begun to insist that their players use stretch exercises to prepare for play. In football, the exercises are called "flexion" or "flex" exercises. They serve the same purpose as stretch exercises do for skaters, loosening and stretching the muscles to make them more responsive, more supple, and stronger. Football trainers find that flex exercises done daily—and before, during, and after games—help to improve the function of the muscles and to lower the injury rate. Trainers claim that as a result of such exercise, some 240-pound linemen can get into a split position. Football players survive those impossible positions they get into with each pileup because their bodies have been there before.

Flex exercises begin with movements designed to get the heart and lungs working at peak capacity. This may be running laps, running in place, or perhaps jumping rope. Thereafter, stretch exercises can be done more easily. For football, stretch exercises are often followed by a weight workout to increase muscle strength.

Some type of warm-up and workout is advisable for skaters, too. When a muscle works, it goes from a longer size to a shorter one. To do this, each cell in the muscle becomes a little shorter. This shortening uses oxygen to burn sugar and release carbon dioxide and water. As the muscle uses sugar and oxygen to contract, heat is given off. This heat improves the efficiency of the contracting muscle, since a muscle works better as it warms up. The chemical reactions that take place in the muscle are more efficient at higher temperatures. Also, the increase in muscle temperature causes an increase in blood flow to the muscle itself, making available more oxygen and sugar and increasing the ability of the blood to remove the byproducts of muscle metabolism.

So a warm-up is literally a method of warming up the muscle to make it work better. It is, of course, possible to provide muscles with a passive warm-up, using a hot bath, hot pack, or sauna. For sports, passive warm-up is generally unnecessary and impractical. Just warming up by increasing physical activity should be enough. This warm-up will be improved by your using a layer of clothing such as a warm-up suit to help retain the body heat generated by exercise. For rink conditions, a warm-up layer of clothing will shorten the time you require for warming up.

How much time is needed? This will depend on the individual skater. She or he will learn from the suppleness and responsiveness of muscles how long to warm up. One indication that warm-up is adequate is the developing of a light sweat. This, of course, will take longer under cold rink conditions than in warmer places such as the locker room.

Warm-up is especially important before competitions and exhibitions, when practice time is limited. Off-ice warm-up will shorten the ice time needed to gain full efficiency. It will lessen the likelihood of injuries such as sprains and cramps.

Here is a suggested warm-up routine for skating. First, run or jog in place for three or four minutes, until your pulse rate goes up to about 120 and a light sweat forms. Then you are ready for stretch exercises.

One basic stretch exercise is familiar—bending at the waist to touch your toes. Start with your feet close together, but then you should gradually move your feet apart, thereby encouraging increased stretching of your back, arm, and leg muscles. Variations of this basic exercise include touching your toes alternately: your right hand to your left toes on one bend, your left hand to your right toes on the next bend, and so on.

Your back muscles can be stretched further by an exercise that includes extending your arms horizontally to your sides and then swiveling your body at the waist, alternately left and right. You should swivel far enough each way to have your arms pointing to front and back of your starting position.

It's useful to lie on your back and do simple leg-raising. Also useful is raising your legs as far as possible while you lie face-down.

If you want to do more stretching exercises, you will discover specific ones for each muscle group of your body, each exercise designed to increase the strength and extension of the appropriate muscles.

After your stretch exercises, put on your boots and take to the ice. Like football players, skaters can expect to survive all their skating positions because their bodies have been there before. Proper warming up is bound to lessen your muscle injuries and improve your skating.

Foot Care

Care of the skater's feet is not different from foot care for other sports. In skating, the feet bear the brunt of the exercise, so it is important that skating boots fit comfortably (see the section on boots).

Break in new skating boots before trying to skate in them. This can be done at home simply by attaching skate guards and walking around the house in your boots. In this way, the boots will begin to mold themselves to your feet at home, leaving one less problem for your next skating session.

Prepare your feet for skating as you would for any other active sport. Toenails should be cut straight across, not curved to the shape of the toe. This minimizes the likelihood of developing painful ingrown toenails. If a nail difficulty develops, have it cared for by a doctor or podiatrist. Never attempt to remove corns, bunions, or calluses surgically yourself.

Foot and ankle exercises may improve the strength, flexibility, and coordination of your feet. One simple exercise involves rolling a soda bottle along the ground with the sole of your bare foot. Another is to grasp a small object such as a pencil or a marble with your toes and lift it off the floor. This should be done often with both feet until facility is developed.

Walking on the inside edges of both feet is an exercise to develop ankle strength. Walking on the outside edge is another. Rising on the toes and walking on them is still another exercise to strengthen the ankle and heel. These exercises should be done for a minute or two, morning and evening, for a few days before the first skating lessons. They are also good warm-up exercises to be done at home before going to the rink.

Only one pair of socks should be worn under a skating boot. The boots themselves provide a great deal of warmth for the foot and are raised almost two inches off the surface of the ice by the blades. Socks should be of average weight; a thick sock tends to reduce the feel of the foot against the ice. For this reason, too, the same weight sock should be worn each time you skate to keep the fit of the boot and the feel of the ice constant.

Street-weight cotton socks are best. Avoid stretch fabrics. They tend to change size and shape, permitting the foot to slide inside the boot and sometimes causing marked chafing.

Athlete's foot is no more a problem for skaters than it is for other athletes. It is treated by keeping the feet perfectly dry and quite clean. Feet tend to sweat more in the closely fitted skating boot, with its high top, than in low-cut and loosely fitted street shoes, so we recommend a change of socks when you switch from skating boots to street shoes. Before you put on clean socks, dry your feet carefully. Powders and sprays available at any drugstore are a big help in the treatment and prevention of athlete's foot.

Frostbite is a problem that sometimes occurs in winter sports. It does not usually happen to indoor skaters, since rink temperatures are usually in the fifties, but is often a problem for people who skate outdoors. Frostbite results from impaired blood circulation. It can happen from skating in extreme cold, or it can happen when you skate in moderate cold while wearing boots that are tight enough to impair the circulation. Properly fitted boots are a precaution against frostbite.

Frostbite is a fine, descriptive, even poetic term. But it is also the medical name for what can happen to the feet in prolonged exposure to cold. Various degrees of frostbite can occur: from mild redness and swelling to severe blistering or even actual death of tissue, called gangrene. It's fortunate that skaters rarely get frostbite, and severe frostbite is almost unheard of.

The best medical management for prevention of frostbite is to avoid unusual exposure to chilling. Properly fitted boots, loose enough to permit good circulation of blood, are essential. For outdoor skating, sometimes it is necessary to use socks that are a little heavier than the ones recommended for indoor skating. It is important to keep the skates, socks, and feet dry, since wetness helps to conduct the body heat away, increasing the likelihood of frostbite. Activity such as stamping the feet on the ice and wiggling the toes is helpful, too. But if tingling, burning, or numbness of the feet develops, it is time to seek shelter and warmth.

Of course, any exposed part of the body can suffer frostbite. Fingers and toes are the common sites, and cheeks and noses are sometimes involved. If signs of frostbite on any part of the body occur while skating, head indoors as soon as possible.

Treatment of frostbite should encourage the gradual return of circulation and normal temperature to the frozen part. Gentle heat may be applied, but never higher than normal skin temperature, which is about 90°. To be safe, in thawing out after frostbite, gentle application of heat at 40 to 60° F. is best, beginning at 40° and increasing gradually. The frostbitten part may be heated with heating pad or warm compresses or immersed in warm water, always starting at 40° F. if possible and increasing the warmth only very gradually.

Remember that these measures are first-aid treatment for frostbite. In the unusual case that true frostbite develops, seek expert medical advice immediately. Even outdoors, frostbite practically never develops in active, well-dressed outdoor skaters.

Some Tips on Teaching Children

It is natural for children to want to learn new things. They will take to skating most eagerly when the idea is their own. Under the stimulus of TV, many children are being exposed to hockey and figure skating. So perhaps a hockey game or ice-show spectacular will provide the incentive for your child to want to learn.

When your child asks about skating, you should be prepared to teach. Read through this whole book first. It contains many tips to make your child's first experience of skating an enjoyable one. The book also contains the answers to many questions that a child may ask about skating, skates, rinks, and the like.

Prepare each skating lesson ahead of time. If you are a skater, try each lesson yourself before attempting to teach it to your child. If you're a nonskater, this is a good opportunity for you to learn. Stay one lesson ahead of your child if you can, but don't be disappointed if you can't. Children generally learn to skate faster than adults do.

When should your child begin? A child who is old enough to walk on skates is old enough to skate. For most children, age five or six is a good time to begin. Some children will be ready before, some not until a year or two later. But most important is the element of interest. A four-year-old child who is interested may well learn faster than an eight-year-old who is not.

Learn to sustain that interest. Do not offer too much at one time. Make sure the child masters each step before going on to the next one. Be free with your praise of his or her progress. Provide encouragement and reassurance at all times.

Do not be upset if the child falls. Falling is a normal part of learning to skate, particularly for children. They take it quite casually, hardly seeming to notice, and rarely hurt themselves.

A relaxed attitude on the part of the parent is most important. After all, skating is just another form of recreation. Nothing very important depends upon your child's success or failure at skating. Most children can learn to skate easily. So carry a relaxed, positive attitude to the rink with you. It will prove an inspiration and stimulus to your child.

Kids like motion, action, new sensations. They'll love learning to skate.

Where Do We Go from Here?

So far, you have learned the basic elements of all kinds of skating. By now you should be able to move forward and backward comfortably on the ice and to corner and turn well, at least in the forward direction. If you have been especially diligent, you can probably do most of these maneuvers backward, too. Probably you have fallen several times, at least often enough to have relieved your fear of falling. Along the way, you have probably noticed experienced skaters who can do more complicated movements on the ice in their various areas of skating.

Perhaps you have recognized as crossovers the pushing movements that figure skaters make before some of their jumps. Maybe you have noticed that hockey players often move around the puck with a motion like the Mohawk. You may have watched speed skaters using the thrust that you learned as a scissor push to generate their speed on crossovers. You have probably seen couples dancing on the ice, using the 3 turn to change position and direction.

In fact, hockey skaters, in their daily drills and games, use most of the techniques you have learned. Figure skaters use all of these motions for their figures and their free skating. Speed skaters are most interested in the refinement of forward motion on the ice for speed, so they use fewer of these techniques, but develop them more highly. Remember that any advanced skater had to begin just as you did, by learning these basic maneuvers.

Once you have the basics in hand, you can look forward to specializing in one or more aspects of skating. Most boys seem to prefer the team contact of hockey. Some boys choose the athletic challenges of speed skating and hockey, but the greatest interest among girls seems to be in the glamor of figure skating.

Ice dancing and couple skating attract a wide range of age groups. Older folks particularly enjoy ice dancing for the moderate rather than strenuous exercise it affords, and for the pleasant social aspects. The largest number of skaters are recreational skaters who learn to enjoy motion on the ice. It is from this group of recreational skaters, particularly the younger ones, that the speed skaters, hockey stars, and figure skaters develop.

So look around for the area of skating that interests you most. See a hockey game. Enjoy a figure-skating competition. Thrill to a speed-skating match. Perhaps try skating with and talking to hockey players, figure skaters, and racers when they turn up at the rink. See how well you relate to what they are doing. Perhaps you would like to specialize as a skater yourself. Enjoy!

Index